A World of Christmas

Holiday Songs, Carols, and Customs from 15 Countries

A Global Songbook or Program for Unison and 2-Part Voices

By Sally K. Albrecht

Recording Orchestrated by Tim Hayden

See back cover for CD Track Numbers.

Performance time: approximately 50 minutes with script (30 music, 20 script).

Note: Reproducible Student Pages and color cover art are included as PDF files on the Enhanced SoundTrax CD.

Book & CD (39964) ISBN-10: 0-7390-9558-7 ISBN-13: 978-0-7390-9558-4
Teacher's Handbook (39962) ISBN-10: 0-7390-9557-9 ISBN-13: 978-0-7390-9557-7
Enhanced SoundTrax CD (39963)

NOTE: The purchase of this book carries with it the right to photocopy the entire book. Limited to one school/organization. NOT FOR RESALE.

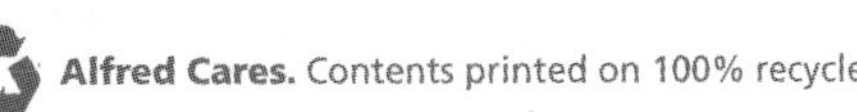
Alfred Cares. Contents printed on 100% recycled paper.

PERFORMANCE NOTES

A World of Christmas is designed to teach young singers about other cultures, customs, languages, and music. Use it as a songbook (approximately 30 minutes) or use the optional script to create a full-fledged global musical (approximately 50 minutes). Feel free to add other favorite holiday songs from other countries, or select only your favorites for a shorter program. You'll see that 10 narrators introduce the customs of each country. Again, feel free to cut back on these lines as you wish. Use the same 10 speakers throughout the program, or change before each song—it's up to you.

If you teach many different classes, consider having all your children perform the opening and closing numbers, with different individual classes performing one or more songs alone.

This program may be performed simply on risers, with narrators coming forward before each selection. Consider using the study of this material to develop further interdisciplinary study:

- Invite a geography teacher to talk about the different countries that are featured: the locations, hemispheres, longitudes and latitudes, major cities, topography, imports and exports, major crops, etc.
- Invite a language specialist to teach a few important words in each country's native language: yes, no, hello, goodbye, bathroom, count from 1-10, please, thank you, etc.
- Invite an art teacher to help students draw a map of the country, the flag, or even children wearing typical costumes of the country. Plan an art project or exhibit based on the particular art styles of the country or specific region.
- Invite a history teacher to talk about past and recent developments in the country's politics, borders, rulers, etc.
- Invite a chef to talk about foods and perhaps cook a typical dish from a few of the countries.
- Invite a banker to show your students currency from each country.
- Invite an ethnomusicologist to demonstrate musical instruments or play examples of folk music from each country.
- Invite a music specialist to talk about and play examples of the music of famous composers from each country.
- Invite a zoologist to talk about each country's native animals and what they eat.
- Invite a meteorologist to talk about each country's climate and typical weather patterns.
- Invite a travel agent to talk about the highlights of each country, things to see and do, how to get there from here. See if you can collect some travel posters for your hallways and classrooms.

ABOUT THE RECORDING

A World of Christmas was recorded by Tim Hayden at Ned's Place Recording Studio in Nashville, TN. The project was mixed by Kent Heckman at Red Rock Recording in Saylorsburg, PA.

Performers include: Jaclyn Brown, Mallory Egly, Lucy Hames, Hannah McGinley, Hannah Peasall, Noah Pope, Hannah Reddick, Anna Grace Stewart, and Sarah Valley (lead).

The **Enhanced SoundTrax CD** offers the following:

- Access to both Full-Performance and Accompaniment recordings (on your CD player).
- Downloadable PDF files of the reproducible Student Pages, Script, and the full-color program/cover/poster (on your computer.) Note: The purchase of this Enhanced CD carries with it the right to display these images on an electronic blackboard in the classroom and/or on an organization's website.

SALLY K. ALBRECHT

Sally K. Albrecht is the Director of School Choral & Classroom Publications for Alfred Music Publishing. She is a popular choral conductor, composer, and clinician, especially known for her work with choral movement.

An annual recipient of the ASCAP Special Music Award since 1987, Sally has over 400 publications in print, including chorals, songbooks, musicals, cantatas, and movement DVDs. Sally has directed and staged the half-time show singers performing during two Florida Citrus Bowls, and has conducted hundreds of honor choir events, including festivals at Lincoln Center, Carnegie Hall, and The Kennedy Center.

Sally received a B.A. from Rollins College with a double major in Music and Theater. From there she moved to the University of Miami, where she received both an M.A. in Drama and an M.M. in Accompanying. Sally and her husband, composer/arranger Jay Althouse, currently enjoy living in Raleigh, North Carolina.

CHRISTMAS GREETINGS IN OTHER LANDS

Consider creating decorative posters with these greetings, including the country's name and perhaps their flag.

Czech Republic	*Veselé Vánoce*
China	*Sheng Dan Kuai Le (Mandarin)* *Seng Dan Fai Lok (Cantonese)*
Denmark	*Glædelig Jul*
Ethiopia	*Melkm Ganna*
Finland	*Hyvää Joulua*
France/Canada	*Joyeux Noël*
Germany	*Fröhliche Weihnachten*
Ghana	*Afishapa*
Greece	*Kala Christougenna*
Hawaii	*Mele Kalikimaka*
India	*Bade Din ki Mubarak*
Indonesia	*Selamat Natal*
Iran	*Kerismas Mobarak (Farsi)*
Ireland	*Nollaig Shona Shuit*
Italy	*Buon Natale*
Japan	*Meri Kurisumasu* *(Meri Kuri—short version)*
Korea	*Sung Tan Chuk Ha*
Lebanese	*Meelad Majeed*
Navajo	*Nizhonigo Keshmish*
New Zealand	*Meri Kirihimete (Maori)*
Nigeria	*Eku Odun Ebi Jesu*
Philippines	*Maligayang Pasko*
Poland	*Boze Narodzenia*
Portugal	*Feliz Natal*
Russia	*S Rozhdestvom Khristovym*
Scotland	*Blithe Yule (Scots)*
Spain/Mexico	*Feliz Navidad*
Sweden/Norway	*God Jul*
Swahili	*Heri ya Krismas*
Switzerland	*Schöni Wiehnachte*
Tahiti	*Ia orana te Noera*
Vietnam	*Chung Mung Giang Sinh*
Wales	*Nadolig Llawen*

WEBSITES OF INTEREST TO VISIT:

freelang.net/expressions/christmas.php
theholidayspot.com/christmas/worldxmas/
santas.net/aroundtheworld.htm
whychristmas.com/cultures
worldofchristmas.net/christmas-world
xmasfun.com

1. A WORLD OF CHRISTMAS

Words and Music by
SALLY K. ALBRECHT

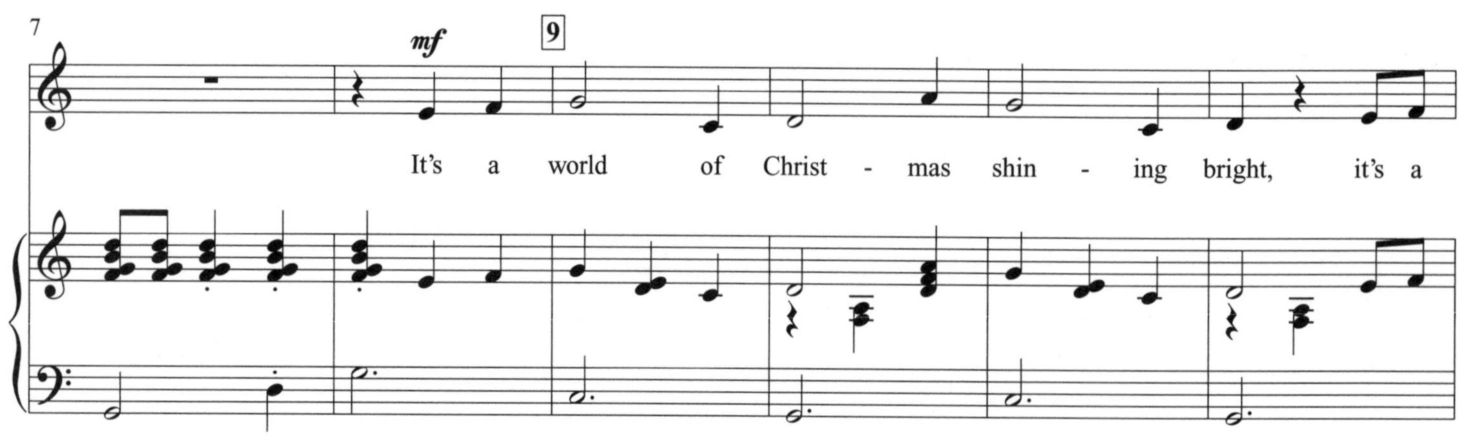

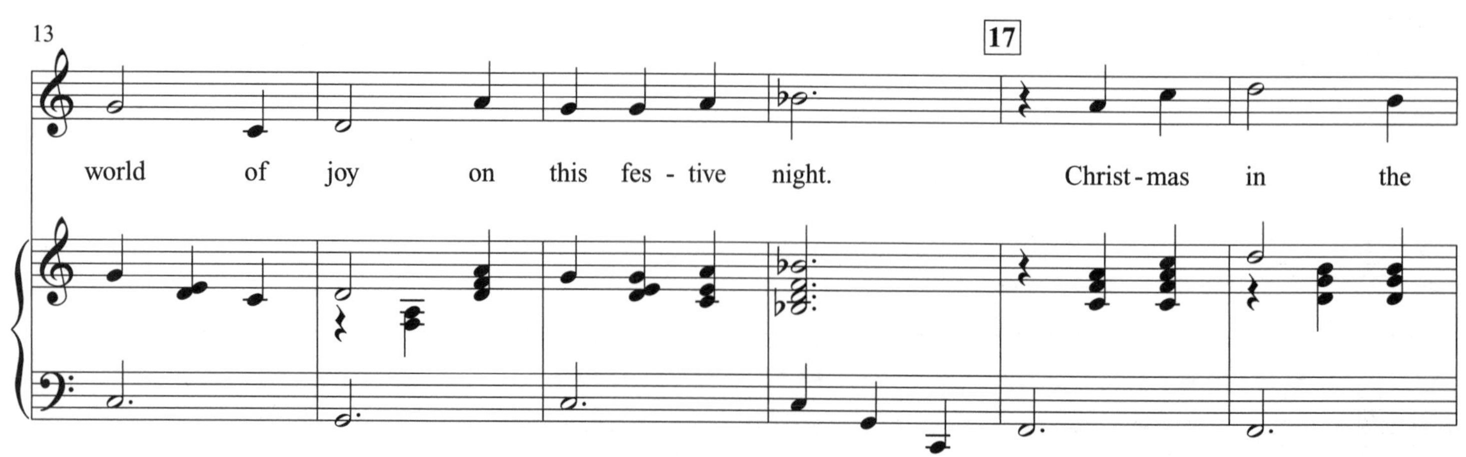

19
24
air!
Christ-mas ev - 'ry - where!
It's a world of
26
Christ - mas far and near,
it's a world of cel - e - bra - tions each
32
33
year.
Christ-mas in the air!
Christ-mas ev - 'ry -
39
41
where!
There are hol - i - day tra - di - tions both young and old.

* loo-mee-nah-ree-ah

69
Christ-mas in the air!
Christ-mas ev - 'ry -
75
77
cresc.
where! It's a won - der-ful, mag - i-cal, mar - vel-ous, glo - ri-ous
cresc.
81
f
world
of Christ-mas,
of
f
87
Christ-mas,
of Christ-mas!

ENGLAND

2. CAROLING ON CHRISTMAS NIGHT

Sussex Carol • Here We Come A-Caroling

English Carols
Arranged by **SALLY K. ALBRECHT**

17
Christ - mas night all chil - dren sing, to hear the news the an - gels bring.
of the dark - ness we have light, which makes the an - gels sing this night.
21
News of great joy and of great mirth. Hear glad tid - ings of the ba - by's
27
1.
2.
birth.
Out
1.
2.
33
Here we come a - car - ol - ing a - mong the leaves so green. Here we come a -

38
41
f
(♩. = 𝅗𝅥)
wan - d'ring, so fair to be seen. Love and joy come to you, and to
43
you good Christ-mas, too. And God bless you and send you a hap - py new
48
(𝅗𝅥 = ♩.)
year. And God send you a hap - py new year.
53
Here we come a - car - ol - ing.

FRANCE

3. TWO FRENCH CAROLS

Sing We Now of Christmas • Pat-A-Pan

French Carols
Arranged, with new Words, by
SALLY K. ALBRECHT

* roundelay (French - rondelet) - a song or poem with a regularly recurring refrain

34
mf
Wil- lie,
41
get your lit - tle drum. Rob- in, get your flute and come. On these in - stru-ments we'll
mf
Pat pat - a - pan pan pan. Pat pat - a - pan pan pan. On these in - stru-ments we'll
46
play. Tu - re - lu - re - lu, pat - a - pat - a - pan. On these in - stru-ments we'll play, for a joy - ful
play. Tu - re - lu - re - lu, pat - a - pat - a - pan. On these in - stru-ments we'll play, for a joy - ful

51
56
Christ - mas day!
Christ - mas day!
Sing we now of
57
mf
decresc. to end
Sing we now of Christ - mas.
Sing we now of
Christ - mas.
decresc. to end
Sing we now of Christ - mas.
decresc. to end
63
Christ - mas.
p
Pat pat - a - pan pan pan.
p
Pat pat - a - pan pan pan.
Pat pat - a - pan pan pan.
p
pp

4. O CHRISTMAS, WE GREET YOU

(O Jul med din Glaede)

Norwegian Carol
Arranged, with English Words, by
SALLY K. ALBRECHT

7
greet you with clap - ping and sing - ing. We raise now our voic - es in
fol - low a star to the sta - ble. So come now to - geth - er, and
greet you with clap - ping and sing - ing. We raise now our voic - es in
fol - low a star to the sta - ble. So come now to - geth - er, and
10
f
song, clear and bright, while bells in the dis - tance are ring - ing. Our
join hand in hand, to sing to the babe in the cra - dle.
f
song, clear and bright, while bells in the dis - tance are ring - ing. Our
join hand in hand, to sing to the babe in the cra - dle.
f
13
hand claps
hands we will clap this day, as mer - ri - ly we say, "We wel - come you this
hands we will clap this day, as mer - ri - ly we say, "We wel - come you this

16
1.
glo - rious day." We sing and dance for joy Christ-mas morn - ing.
glo - rious day." We sing and dance for joy Christ-mas morn - ing.
1.
mf
19
2.
20
morn - ing. Our hands we will clap this day, as mer - ri - ly we say, "We
morn - ing. Our hands we will clap this day, as mer - ri - ly we say, "We
2.
22
wel - come you this Christ - mas day!"
wel - come you this Christ - mas day!"
ff

CZECH REPUBLIC

5. ROCKING CAROL

Czech Carol
Arranged, with new Words, by
SALLY K. ALBRECHT

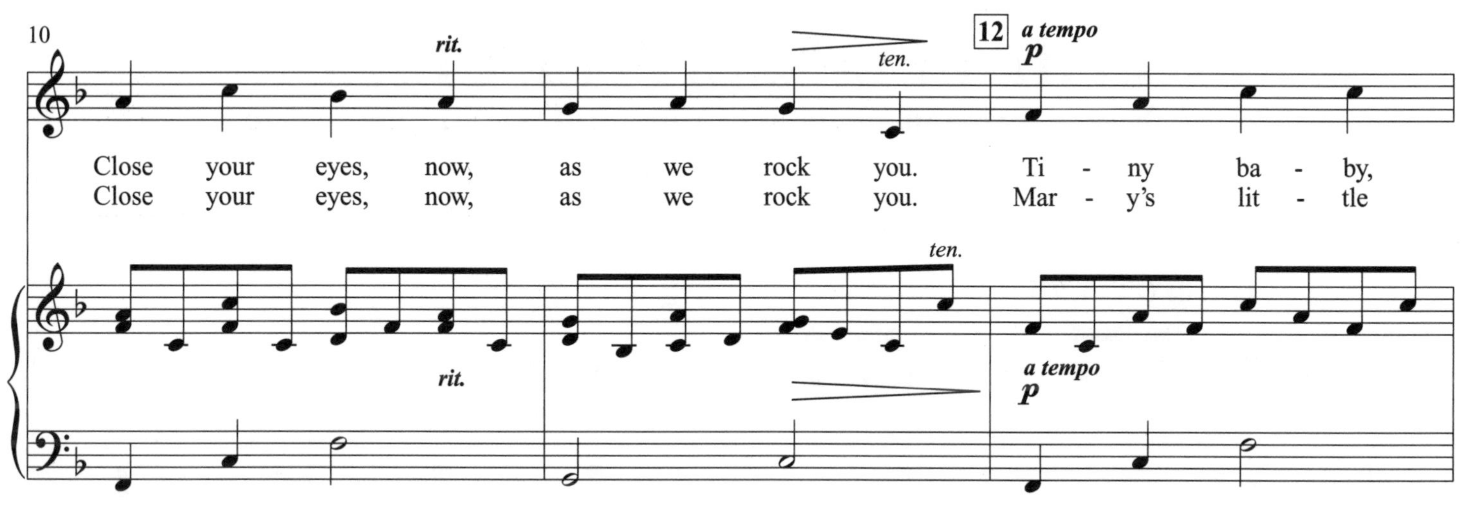
10
rit.
ten.
12
a tempo
p
Close your eyes, now, as we rock you. Ti - ny ba - by,
Close your eyes, now, as we rock you. Mar - y's lit - tle
ten.
rit.
a tempo
p

13
rit.
sweet - ly sleep. Slum - ber gent - ly, do not weep.
ba - by boy, filled with glad - ness, filled with joy.
rit.

16
a tempo
rit.
Sleep, sleep, sleep.
a tempo
rit.
pp

GERMANY

6. RING THE BELLS, LITTLE CHILDREN

Ring, Christmas Bells • O Come, Little Children

German Carols
Arranged, with additional English Words, by
SALLY K. ALBRECHT

* close quickly to "ng"

13
17
Ring bells, oh ring-a-ling-a-ling.
Kling, kling, kling, oh
19
Ring Christ-mas bells! Win-ter-time is call-ing, snow is soft-ly
ring Christ-mas bells! Win-ter-time is call-ing, snow is soft-ly
24
25
fall-ing. Hear the bells a-ring-ing, joy-ful-ly they're sing-ing.
fall-ing. Hear the bells a-ring-ing, joy-ful-ly they're sing-ing.

29
33
Ring bells, oh ring-a-ling-a-ling. Ring Christ-mas bells! Kling-e-ling-e-ling,
Kling, kling, kling, oh ring Christ-mas bells! Kling,
34
kling-e-ling-e-ling, ring those Christ-mas bells! Kling-e-ling-e-ling,
kling, ring those Christ-mas bells! Kling,
38
kling-e-ling-e-ling, ring those Christ-mas bells!
kling, ring those Christ-mas bells!
cresc.

43
45
f
O come, lit - tle chil - dren. O come, one and all. O
Kling, kling, kling, oh ring Christ-mas bells!
49
53
come to the cra - dle in Beth - le - hem's stall. Come see what has
Kling, kling, kling, oh ring Christ - mas bells! Come see what has
54
hap - pened on this spe - cial night. Come gaze on the child, filled with

59
61
mf
love and de - light.
Ring bells, oh
mf
love and de - light. O come, lit - tle chil - dren.
mf
64
mp
ring-a-ling-a-ling.
Ring bells, oh ring-a-ling-a-ling.
mp
O come, lit - tle chil - dren.
mp
69
cresc. to end
Come, come, come.
cresc. to end
Come, come, come.
cresc. to end
ff

POLAND

7. COME NOW, REJOICING
(Dzisiaj w Betlejem)

Polish Carol
Arranged, with English Words, by
SALLY K. ALBRECHT

13
mf
An - gels are sing - ing, No - els they're bring - ing. Wise men are pray - ing, shep - herds are say - ing,
mf
An - gels are sing - ing, No - els they're bring - ing. Wise men are pray - ing, shep - herds are say - ing,
mf
17
"Glo - ry hal - le - lu - jah, glo - ry hal - le - lu - jah, come, re - joic - ing, on this
"Glo - ry hal - le - lu - jah, glo - ry hal - le - lu - jah, come, re - joic - ing, on this
21
1.
2.
rit.
day."
day."
day."
day."
1.
2.
decresc.
decresc.
rit.
mp

8. FUM, FUM, FUM

Spanish Carol
Arranged, with English Words, by
SALLY K. ALBRECHT

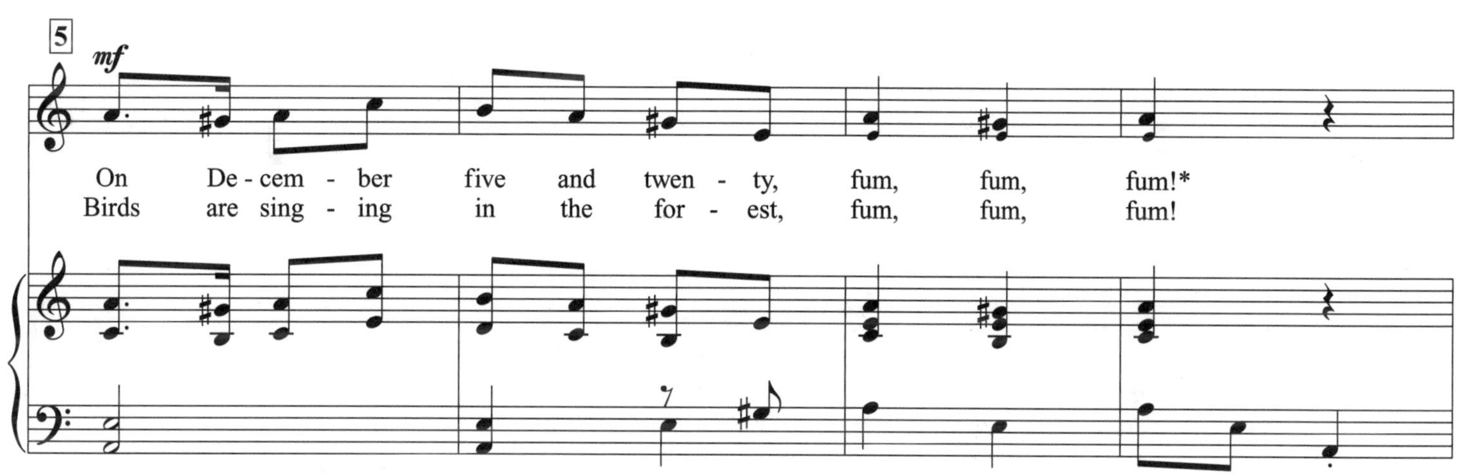

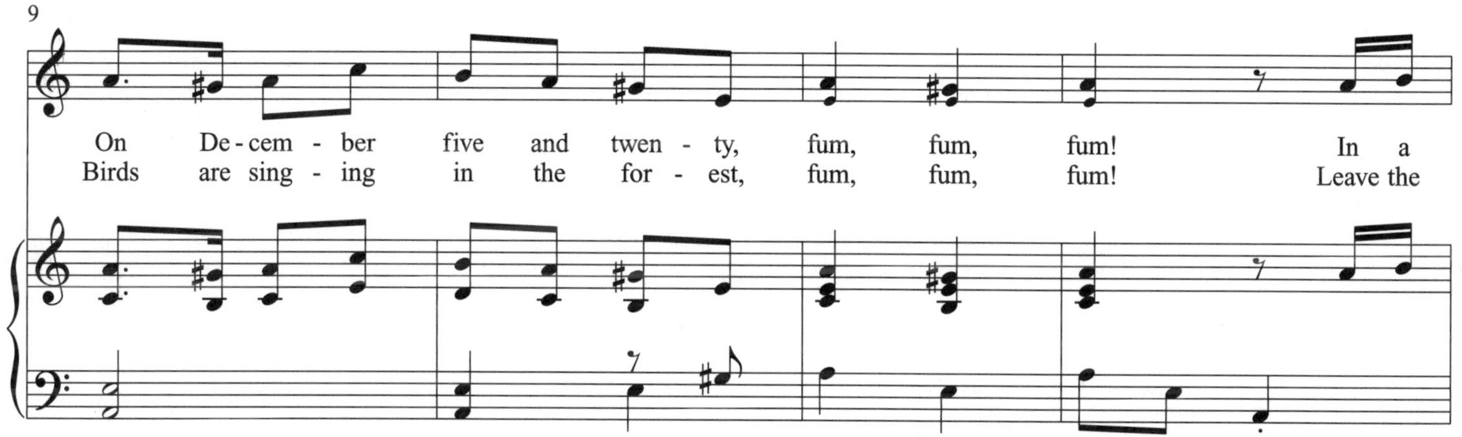

* foom (representing the strum of a guitar)

13
man - ger born this night, the ti - ny babe, the child of
ti - ny ones at home, they will be safe, they will not
16
light. In the sta - ble he lay sleep - ing, moth - er
roam. Come and build a nest in - stead where lit - tle
19
Mar - y watch was keep - ing, fum, fum, fum!
Christ may rest his head, sing fum, fum, fum!
(babe)
22
f
Sing fum, fum, fum!
cresc.
f

AUSTRIA

9. A STILL, SILENT NIGHT

Still, Still, Still • Silent Night

Austrian Carols

Arranged by **SALLY K. ALBRECHT**

10
soft - ly___ sing - ing. Heav - en - ly an - gel voic - es___ ring - ing. Still,___ still,___
soft - ly___ sing - ing. Heav - en - ly an - gel voic - es___ ring - ing. Still, still,
14
molto rit.
Sweetly (♪ = ca. 88)
still, the___ ba - by___ sleeps to - night.
still, the ba - by sleeps to - night.
Sweetly (♪ = ca. 88)
molto rit.
decresc.
18
(optional audience sing-along)
p
Si - lent night, ho - ly night. All is calm, all is bright.
p
Si - lent night, ho - ly night. All is calm, all is bright.
p

22
'Round yon vir - gin moth - er and child. Ho - ly in - fant, so ten - der and mild.
'Round yon vir - gin moth - er and child. Ho - ly in - fant, so ten - der and mild.
26
mp
Sleep in heav - en-ly peace, sleep in heav - en-ly peace.
mp
Sleep in heav - en-ly peace, in heav - en-ly peace, in heav - en-ly peace.
mp
decresc.
30
rit.
p
pp
Still, still, peace.
p
pp
Peace, peace.
rit.
p
pp

ITALY

10. CAROL OF THE BAGPIPERS
(Canzone di Zampognari)

Italian Carol
Arranged, with English Words, by
SALLY K. ALBRECHT

* close quickly to "m"

8
born. It shone a ra - diant light, turn - ing
earth. The world re - joiced and sang of the
brum, brum. Brum, brum,
11
13
dark - ness in - to morn.
ba - by's hum - ble birth.
Star shin - ing bright - ly, ev - er so
brum, brum, brum. Star shin - ing bright - ly, ev - er so
14
light - ly. Come to the sta - ble, fol - low the light. Three
light - ly. Come to the sta - ble, fol - low the light.

17
wise men fol - lowed that star. Its bright - ness led them
Fol - lowed that star. Brum,
20
from a - far ___ to ___ see the won - drous sight.
brum, brum, brum, brum.
24
rit. (2nd time only)
1.
mf
2.
And
1.
2.
rit. (2nd time only)

11. AN AFRICAN CELEBRATION

Betelehemu • African Noel

African Folk Songs
Arranged by **SALLY K. ALBRECHT**

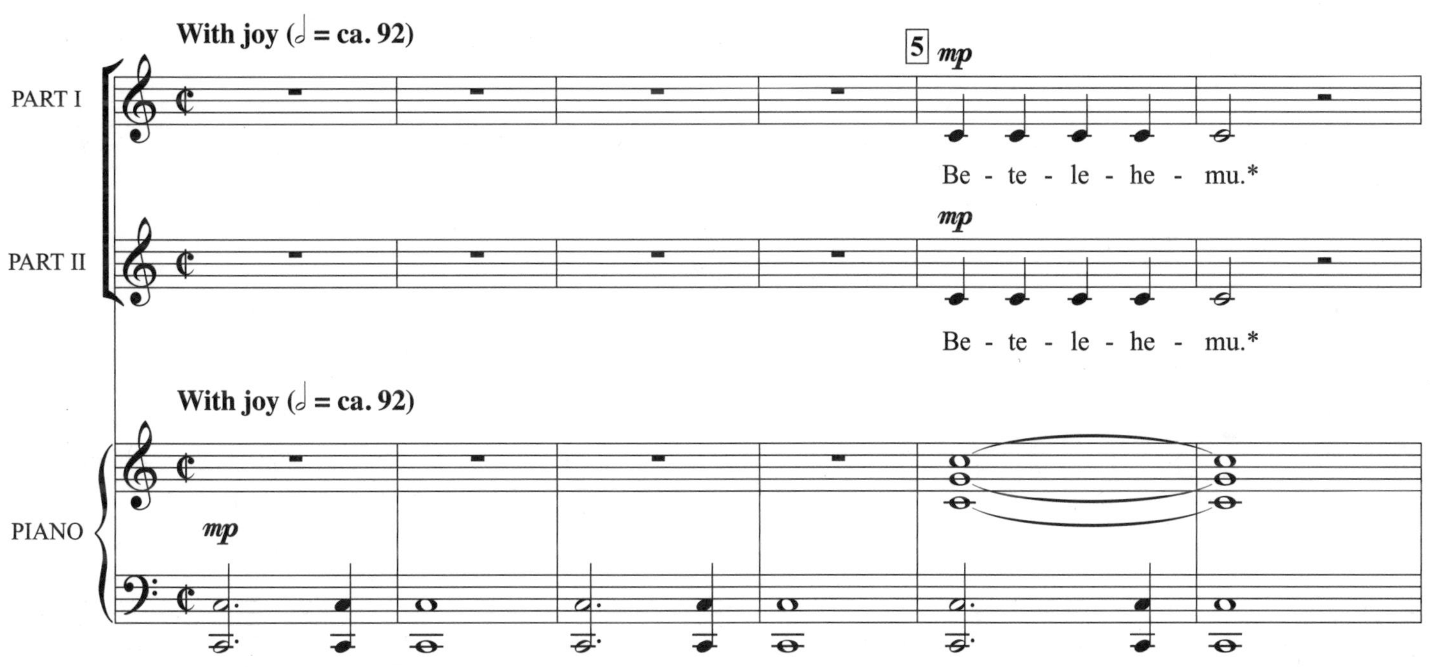

* Beh-teh-leh-heh-moo

13
Sing we all No - el. Sing we all No - el. Sing we all No - el.
Be - te - le - he - mu. Be - te - le - he - mu. Be - te - le - he - mu.
19
cresc.
Sing we all No - el. Sing al - le - lu - ia.
cresc.
Be - te - le - he - mu. Sing al - le - lu - ia.
cresc.
25
mf
Sing No - el, sing No - el, No - el, No - el. Sing No - el, sing No - el,
mf
Sing No - el, sing No - el, No - el, No - el. Sing No - el, sing No - el,
mf

31
33
No - el, No - el.
Sing No - el,
sing No - el,
No - el, No - el.
No - el, No - el.
Sing No - el,
sing No - el,
No - el, No - el.
37
41
f
Sing No - el,
sing No - el,
No - el, No - el.
Sing we all No -
Sing No - el,
sing No - el,
No - el, No - el.
f
42
el.
Sing we all No - el.
Sing we all No - el.
f
Be - te - le - he - mu.
Be - te - le - he - mu.
Be - te - le - he -

47
49
Sing we all No - el.
Sing No - el,
sing No - el,
No - el, No - el.
mu.
Be - te - le - he - mu.
Sing No - el,
No - el, No - el.
53
57
decresc.
Sing No - el,
sing No - el,
No - el, No - el.
Sing No - el,
sing No - el,
decresc.
Sing No - el,
sing No - el,
No - el, No - el.
Sing No - el,
sing No - el,
decresc.
59
No - el, No - el.
Sing No - el,
sing No - el,
No - el, No - el.
No - el, No - el.
Sing No - el,
sing No - el,
No - el, No - el.

65
mp
Be - te - le - he - mu. Be - te - le - he - mu. Be - te - le - he -
mp
Be - te - le - he - mu. Be - te - le - he - mu. Be - te - le - he -
mp
70
mu. Be - te - le - he - mu. Sing al - le - lu -
cresc.
mu. Be - te - le - he - mu. Sing al - le - lu -
cresc.
cresc.
76
i - a! Sing we all No - el.
f
i - a! Sing we all No - el.
f
f

RUSSIA

12. DEDUSHKA MOROZ

Russian Folk Song "Kalinka"
Arranged, with new Words, by
SALLY K. ALBRECHT

* Deh-doo-shkah Moh-rohz

* bah-lah-li-kah (i = as in eye), peh-reh-plee-ahs

VENEZUELA

13. DIN, DIN, DIN
(The Journey)

Venezuelan Carol
Arranged, with new Words, by
SALLY K. ALBRECHT

* deen (close quickly to the "n") - imitating the sound of bells

16
side. Slow-ly they moved on - ward, Jo-seph as her guide.
way. Slow-ly they moved on - ward, till the end of day.
21
23
mp
Friends had gath-ered 'round them as they left their
decresc.
mp
26
home - land. Now they were a - lone, and look-ing for some rest.
31
Sun-light rays were dy - ing, as they looked for shel - ter. But no one would

36
39
mf
help them, hope-less was their quest.
Din, din, din,
mf
41
we must be on our way.
Din, din, din,
this is the cho - sen
46
47
day.
Mar-y on her don - key, Jo-seph by her side.
Slow-ly they moved
52
rit. e decresc.
on - ward, Jo-seph as her guide.
rit. e decresc.
p

MEXICO

14. THE SEARCH FOR A ROOM

(Pedida de Posada)

Mexican Carol
Arranged, with new Words, by
SALLY K. ALBRECHT

13
We are so wea - ry, have mer - cy on us, we pray.
How do we know you won't rob us and run a - way?
17
We need some shel - ter, but we are not a - ble to
Please go a - way. You must find some - where else you can
21
pay.
stay.
1st verse SOLO/SMALL GROUP
2nd verse ALL
27
mf
Please, won't you give us a room? Do you have a spare?
Jo - seph, dear Jo - seph, this house, it is not an inn.

31

We have been trav - 'ling all day. Have you one to share?
But we are hap - py to let both of you come in.

35

We are so wea - ry, have mer - cy on us, we pray. We need some
We are so hon - ored to serve you this ho - ly night. En - ter, we

40

rit. (2nd time only)
shel - ter, but we are not a - ble to pay.
beg you, and keep Mar - y close in your sight.
rit. (2nd time only)

CANADA

15. HURON CAROL

(Jesous Ahatonhia)

English translation by
JESSE EDGAR MIDDLETON (1927)

Canadian Carol
Arranged, with additional Words, by
SALLY K. ALBRECHT

* Huron Indian term for "Supreme Deity"

16
mp
18
Be - fore their light the stars grew dim, and
But as the hunt - er braves drew nigh, the
an - gel choirs in - stead.
wrapped his beau - ty round.
Drum, drum, drum, drum, drum, drum,
20
22
mf
wan-d'ring hun - ters heard the hymn.
an - gel's song rang loud and high.
Wel-come your new-born king. Come forth and
mf
drum, drum, drum, drum drum, drum. Wel-come your new-born king. Come forth and
mf
25
rit.
sing. "In ex - cel - sis glo - ri - a!"
sing. "In ex - cel - sis glo - ri - a!"
mp
rit.

UNITED STATES

16. SHEPHERDS, GO TELL!

Rise Up, Shepherd • Go, Tell It on the Mountain

American Spirituals
Arranged by **SALLY K. ALBRECHT**

9
Go, tell it on the moun - tain.
lead to the place where the Sav - ior's born.
babe is
13
Rise up, shep-herd,
fol - low,
Rise up, shep-herd,
and fol - low,
17
decresc.
fol - low.
19
mf
Go, tell it on the moun - tain,
decresc.
fol - low.
mf
Go, tell it on the moun - tain,
decresc.
mf

21
o - ver the hills and ev - 'ry - where. Go, tell it on the moun - tain that
a
o - ver the hills and ev - 'ry - where. Go, tell it on the moun - tain that
a
25
27
mp
Je - sus Christ is born.
ti - ny babe
Leave your fields and leave your lambs.
Je - sus Christ is born.
ti - ny babe
mp
29
mf
Rise up, shep- herd, and fol - low.
mp
Leave your sheep and leave your rams.
mf
Rise up, shep- herd, and fol - low.
mf
mp

33
mf
Rise up, shep-herd,
fol - low,
mf
Rise up, shep-herd,
and fol - low,
mf
37
39
fol - low.
f
fol - low.
There's a star in the east on Christ-mas morn.
f
41
f
Rise up, shep-herd, and fol - low.
Rise up, shep-herd, and fol - low. It will lead to the place where the Sav - ior's born.
babe is

45
47
Rise up, shep-herd, and fol-low.
Fol - low, fol - low.
Rise up, shep-herd, and fol-low.
Fol - low, fol - low.
49
Rise up, shep-herd, and fol - low.
Fol-low the star of Beth - le - hem.
Rise up, shep-herd, and fol - low.
Fol - low, fol - low.
53
mf
decresc.
Rise up, shep-herd,
fol-low,
mf
decresc.
Rise up, shep-herd,
and fol-low,
fol-low.
mf
decresc.

Optional Reprise/Bows:
Segue to **1. A World of Christmas.** *Sing from top through m. 40. Take bows from m. 41-59. Sing along from m. 60 to end.*

A World of Christmas

Optional Reproducible Script

By Sally K. Albrecht

Use this optional, reproducible script as an educational and easy way to create a global program. There are ten narrators featured before each musical selection. Use the same speakers throughout, or select a different group for each scene. This reproducible script is also included as a PDF file on the Enhanced SoundTrax CD.

1. A World of Christmas

NARRATOR 1: I just can't wait for Christmas . . . to visit Santa Claus, decorate our tree, sing carols, open presents . . .

NARRATOR 2: Well, you'll just have to wait a little bit longer, because today we're going to celebrate Christmas around the globe . . . and that may take us a minute or two!

NARRATOR 1: How are we going to do that?

NARRATOR 3: By using the universal language of the world.

NARRATOR 1: What language is that?

NARRATOR 3: The language of music. Music can tell us a lot about the people of a country: how they speak, how they live, what kind of melodies and rhythms they like . . .

NARRATOR 4: We're going to sing holiday songs from lots of different countries, and learn about the customs and traditions that happen this time of year.

NARRATOR 1: That's so cool! It's like traveling without having to pack! Where are we going first?

NARRATOR 5: I say we start with England, then work our way around the world from there. The people of England celebrate Yuletide with many traditions that include placing holly and ivy in the window, to protect against evil, . . .

NARRATOR 6: . . . and hanging mistletoe in the doorway! Any guy may claim a kiss from any girl who happens to stand underneath it. The custom is to remove a berry from the mistletoe and give it to the girl. When all the berries are gone, no more kisses!

NARRATOR 7: Kids in England hang stockings or pillowcases at the end of their bed, hoping that Father Christmas will leave a present or two on Christmas Eve.

NARRATOR 8: On December 26th, the people in England, as well as Australia, New Zealand, and parts of Canada, celebrate Boxing Day.

NARRATOR 1: Really? They put on boxing gloves and fight?

NARRATOR 9: *(laughing)* No, that's not it! Originally, churches had small boxes made of clay where people donated money. At the end of Boxing Day, it was broken open, and the money was distributed to the poor.

NARRATOR 10: Now it's a day when employers give their workers a special gift or bonus . . . and a day off!

NARRATOR 1: Well, let's eat some plum pudding, and start the festivities!

2. Caroling on Christmas Night — England

(Sussex Carol • Here We Come A-Caroling)

NARRATOR 1: Let's cross the English Channel and head over to France!

NARRATOR 2: Did you know that *Noël (noh-EHL)* is the French word for "Christmas?"

NARRATOR 3: And French carols are also known as *Noëls.* At first, they were solemn hymns, but later on many became more lively and festive.

NARRATOR 4: After midnight Mass, most families have a big feast called *le Réveillon (luh reh-veh-YOHN),* meaning "the awakening"—to keep everyone awake into the night.

NARRATOR 5: And, after the feast, it's customary to leave a candle burning bright, as a sign to help light the way for Mary and Joseph's arrival.

NARRATOR 6: But the most important symbol of French Christmas is the *crèche (krehsh)* or manger scene. It can be small and simple or large and ornate.

NARRATOR 7: Often, the family *crèche* is handed down from generation to generation. But additional figures, called *santons (sahn-TOHN),* may be added each year.

NARRATOR 8: On Christmas Eve, children leave their shoes sitting by the fireplace, to be filled with goodies by *Père Noël (pehr noh-EHL).*

NARRATOR 9: *Père Noël* also hangs fruits, nuts, tiny toys, and bows on the tree while he's there.

NARRATOR 10: And here's the coolest thing—any child who sends *Père Noël* a letter gets a postcard back in response! It's been an official law there since 1962!

NARRATOR 1: If you're in France this Christmas Eve, don't forget to leave a snack by the fireplace for *Père Noël* . . . oh, and a carrot in your shoe for his donkey!

3. Two French Carols — France

(Sing We Now of Chrismas • Pat-A-Pan)

NARRATOR 1: Winter in Scandinavia is a time of freezing cold and extreme darkness.

NARRATOR 2: The sun is at its greatest distance from the equator, and the days grow shorter and shorter until the arrival of the winter solstice, or *Jul (yoohl)*—meaning "the change."

NARRATOR 3: Saint *Lucia (loo-SEE-ah)* Day announces the beginning of the Christmas season and brighter days ahead.

NARRATOR 4: Early on the morning of December 13th, a daughter from each family puts on a white robe with a red ribbon sash, and a crown made of evergreens and candles.

NARRATOR 5: Together with the "star boys," dressed in long white shirts and pointed hats, they wake their parents, serving coffee and *Lucia* buns known as *lussekatter (loo-seh-KAH-tehr).*

NARRATOR 6: In parts of Scandinavia, a little mischievous gnome or *nisse (NEE-seh)* arrives at Christmas time. He comes at midnight, riding a goat!

NARRATOR 7: He guards the farm animals and plays tricks on children, especially if they forget to leave him a bowl of porridge in the barn.

NARRATOR 8: Ornaments made of straw, blue and white porcelain plates, and hand-dipped candles are among the traditional Scandinavian gifts.

NARRATOR 9: And there's one more incredible gift. Each year since 1947, a giant 70-foot tall Norwegian spruce tree has been sent from the city of Oslo to stand in London's Trafalgar Square.

NARRATOR 10: Finally, on January 13th, Saint Knut's Day is celebrated. It's the end of the month-long holiday season.

NARRATOR 1: The Christmas trees are piled high and become part of a giant bonfire, symbolizing the triumph of light over darkness.

4. O Christmas, We Greet You (O Jul med din Glaede) — Scandinavia

NARRATOR 1: Prague, the capital and largest city of the Czech Republic, has a famous and impressive Christmas Market each year.

NARRATOR 2: Thousands of visitors come during the holidays to buy hand-made gifts, nativity scenes, and holiday decorations.

NARRATOR 3: The most amazing sight happens on the evening of December 5th, the eve of Saint *Mikulas (MEE-koo-lahs)* Day.

NARRATOR 4: It is said that Saint *Mikulas* descends to earth from heaven on a golden rope, wearing a white robe. He's joined on earth by an angel and a devil.

NARRATOR 5: This trio may visit your home, or you may find them roaming around the Old Town Square while children gaze in awe.

NARRATOR 6: Saint *Mikulas* asks each child if they've been good during the past year. Usually, parents have a list handy of the things their child did right . . . and wrong.

NARRATOR 7: Children who have been good are asked to sing a song or recite a poem, after which the angel rewards them with sweets or a small toy.

NARRATOR 8: But if *Mikulas* suspects a child has been naughty, the devil has a sack of black coal or hard potatoes handy.

NARRATOR 9: Or the devil may jokingly threaten to put the child into his sack, to be taken away and straightened out!

NARRATOR 10: Following a day of fasting, the actual feast of Christmas is quiet and peaceful, as the day brings an end to any quarrels or misunderstandings.

5. Rocking Carol — Czech Republic

NARRATOR 1: There is a special magic about Christmas in Germany, a country that has shared so many of its traditions with the world.

NARRATOR 2: The German celebration lasts 45 days, from Saint Andrew's Night at the end of November through the middle of January.

NARRATOR 3: It was in Germany that the custom of decorating a Christmas tree began. Since the early 1600s, trees have been decorated with fruits, foil, and colored paper.

NARRATOR 4: Traditionally, only the adults decorate the tree. They ring a bell when they're ready to reveal the fully-lit and magical tree to their children.

NARRATOR 5: Gingerbread houses began as a German tradition, and the first candy canes were created there in the shape of a shepherd's crook.

NARRATOR 6: The Advent calendar also originated in Germany, featuring 24 little windows, one opened for each day, revealing a special drawing or treat.

NARRATOR 7: On December 5th, children leave their shoes or boots outside the door in the snow, hoping to find a present from Saint Nicholas in the morning.

NARRATOR 8: Handmade nutcrackers and other wooden toys are sold in the Christmas markets, which take over almost every city's main square.

NARRATOR 9: One of the earliest German carols, "Good King Wenceslas," tells the story of a kind king, encouraging all people to treat each other well.

NARRATOR 10: On Christmas Eve, a female angel named *Christkind (KRIHST-kihnt)* flies from house to house, dressed in white with glittering gold wings, tinkling a little bell, and leaving presents for good children.

6. Ring the Bells, Little Children — Germany

(Ring, Christmas Bells • O Come, Little Children)

NARRATOR 1: The Polish people have many wonderful Christmas traditions, starting with the arrival of *Mikolaj (mee-KOH-wee)* on December 6th, dressed in his bishop's robes.

NARRATOR 2: He visits children, giving them small gifts for being good and reminding them of the gifts given to the child by the Three Kings.

NARRATOR 3: As soon as the first star appears on Christmas Eve, family members share *oplatki (oh-PWAHT-kee),* thin wafers decorated with scenes of the nativity.

NARRATOR 4: One person at a time breaks and shares his wafer, signifying friendship and good wishes for the other members of the family.

NARRATOR 5: These treasured wafers are even sent in letters to friends and family, just like mailing Christmas cards.

NARRATOR 6: In many homes, a layer of straw is placed under a white tablecloth for the Christmas meal, representing the manger.

NARRATOR 7: And an extra place is often set for any unexpected visitor, showing that anyone seeking shelter is welcome in this place.

NARRATOR 8: The special midnight Mass is called *Pasterka (pah-STEHR-kah),* or "Shepherd's Watch Mass."

NARRATOR 9: On Christmas, a "Mother Star" delivers gifts to children who have behaved well throughout the year.

NARRATOR 10: During the week between Christmas and New Year, small traveling puppet-theaters called *szopki (SHAHP-kee)* travel across town, featuring scenes from the life of Christ.

7. Come Now, Rejoicing **Poland**
(Dzisiaj w Betlejem)

NARRATOR 1: Celebrations in Spain begin on *Nochebuena (noh-cheh-BWEH-nah),* Christmas Eve, as tiny oil lamps are lit in every house.

NARRATOR 2: Church bells ring throughout the towns and villages, calling people to midnight Mass.

NARRATOR 3: After the service, the streets fill up with people doing a special dance called the *Jota (HOH-tah),* accompanied by guitars, tambourines, and castanets.

NARRATOR 4: Almost every home features a nativity scene or *nacimiento (nah-see-mee-EHN-toh),* around which family members sing songs and carols, called *villancicos (vee-yahn-SEE-kohs).*

NARRATOR 5: There's a large bowl called the "Urn of Fate." Each family member draws one name from the bowl, then must be a devoted friend to that person for the coming year.

NARRATOR 6: On Christmas Day, many children play "Swinging the Sun" on swing sets assembled in public squares. They encourage the sun to move higher and higher into the sky with them during the winter solstice.

NARRATOR 7: Most Spanish children write their wish lists to the Three Kings, receiving their gifts on January 6th, the feast of the Epiphany.

NARRATOR 8: Children leave their shoes filled with straw outside the door, on a balcony, or on a windowsill the night before, often along with three dishes of food for the Kings.

NARRATOR 9: Each child hopes that the Three Kings will find the shoes, use the straw to feed their weary camels, and fill the shoes with gifts.

NARRATOR 10: The grand finale in Spain is on the Epiphany, when a special parade of kings, animals, and children occurs up and down the streets.

8. Fum, Fum, Fum **Spain**

NARRATOR 1: Festivities begin in Austria on December 5th, Krampus Day. Krampus is a devilish figure, dressed in fur and running through the streets creating chaos.

NARRATOR 2: In good fun, both children and adults tease him and laugh at him, pelting him with snowballs and chasing him away.

NARRATOR 3: His true purpose is to remind children to behave well, as Saint Nicholas will arrive the following day.

NARRATOR 4: On Christmas Eve, *Turmblasen (TOORM-blah-sehn)* or "tower-blowers" climb with their brass instruments to the highest city tower or church steeple, playing festive music.

NARRATOR 5: Singers, carrying blazing torches and a manger scene, move from house to house, singing carols as they make their way to the steps of the church.

NARRATOR 6: It was here in Austria that the world's best-known carol, "Silent Night," was first sung in 1818.

NARRATOR 7: Joseph Mohr, a priest at Saint Nicholas Church in Oberndorf, wrote the simple poem, *"Stille Nacht" (SHTIH-leh nahkt),* after blessing a newborn baby on the morning of Christmas Eve.

NARRATOR 8: The priest showed the poem to his friend, Franz Gruber, who was a teacher and church organist.

NARRATOR 9: A few hours later, the melody was written, but the parishioners at Saint Nicholas had a problem—their church organ was currently out of order.

NARRATOR 10: The two men and the church choir held a brief rehearsal, then performed *"Stille Nacht"* that night, accompanied only by guitar.

NARRATOR 1: Now it's a special tradition in Austria: this carol is never heard until Christmas Eve.

9. A Still, Silent Night **Austria**
(Still, Still, Still • Silent Night)

NARRATOR 1: In Italy, the Christmas celebration begins nine days before Christmas, the period known as *novena (noh-VEH-nah).*

NARRATOR 2: During this festive time, children travel from house to house, reciting Christmas poems and singing—in return for coins.

NARRATOR 3: Shepherds come down into the villages, carrying torches as they process, and singing carols accompanied by bagpipes.

NARRATOR 4: In some areas, a large yule log, called a *ceppo (CHEH-poh),* is lit in the fireplace. Children hit the log with sticks, creating sparks that fly up the chimney.

NARRATOR 5: The first nativity scene, called a *presepio (preh-ZEH-pee-oh),* was made in Italy by St. Francis of Assisi. Today, most Italian homes and churches have one.

NARRATOR 6: But you shouldn't place the figure of the baby into this scene until the clock strikes midnight on Christmas Eve!

NARRATOR 7: The well-known fruitcake or *panettone (pan-eh-TOHN-eh)* is a once-a-year specialty in Italy. It's easy to make, and it's durable, lasting for weeks!

NARRATOR 8: On the night of January 6th, presents are received from *La Befana (lah beh-FAHN-ah).* She's a cheerful, tiny, old woman dressed in black.

NARRATOR 9: The story goes that *La Befana* missed going with the Three Kings to visit the baby, because she was too busy sweeping her house at the time.

NARRATOR 10: When she tried to join them later, she couldn't find them or the star. She lost her way, and has been constantly flying around on her broomstick looking for the baby ever since!

10. Carol of the Bagpipers (Canzone di Zampognari) **Italy**

NARRATOR 1: Holiday festivities in Africa differ from country to country. Remember that in parts of Africa, as in the Middle East, Asia, and other places around the world, many people don't celebrate Christmas.

NARRATOR 2: In Ethiopia, Christmas is observed on January 7th with a very early morning service. Upon entering the church, each person receives a candle.

NARRATOR 3: Once all the candles have been lit, the people process around the church three times before the service begins.

NARRATOR 4: Twelve days later, Ethiopians begin the three-day celebration of *Timkat, (TEEM-kaht)* commemorating the baptism of Christ. Priests wear turbans and carry large embroidered and fringed umbrellas.

NARRATOR 5: In Egypt, Santa may be seen riding a camel to deliver presents!

NARRATOR 6: Palm trees in Liberia are decorated with beautiful red bells, and spectacular evening fireworks light up the sky.

NARRATOR 7: In Ghana, the Christmas season coincides with the huge cocoa harvest. And Father Christmas doesn't travel from the North Pole, but from the jungle!

NARRATOR 8: Children in Nigeria process from house to house in costumes, holding sparklers, and acting out the nativity story in return for coins, which they donate to the poor.

NARRATOR 9: In the Congo, the day begins with an annual Christmas pageant as carolers walk through the village, each person bringing a small gift to the morning service.

NARRATOR 10: And in South Africa, it's the time of the summer holiday! Warm weather greets Father Christmas as he arrives with gifts on Christmas Eve.

11. An African Celebration — Africa

(Betelehemu (Nigeria) • African Noel)

NARRATOR 1: Christmas arrives in Russia with many joyous traditions, and is celebrated on January 7th.

NARRATOR 2: On Christmas Eve, as the first star appears in the evening sky, families gather around their table to join in "The Holy Supper."

NARRATOR 3: A white tablecloth is used, in tribute to the baby's swaddling cloths.

NARRATOR 4: And hay is spread on the floors and tables, reminding the family of the humble stall where the baby was born.

NARRATOR 5: A special porridge called *kutia (KOO-tee-ah)* is served. It's made of grains, honey, poppy seeds, and fruits, and is often eaten from a common bowl, to symbolize unity.

NARRATOR 6: Some families throw a spoonful of *kutia* up on the ceiling. If it sticks there, that means good luck and good harvest for the coming year.

NARRATOR 7: Later in the day, families may take a ride together in a *troika (TROY-kah),* a sleigh pulled by three horses.

NARRATOR 8: In Russia, many additional customs occur on New Year's Eve, the night the pine tree, called a *yolka (YOHL-kah),* is cut and trimmed with homemade fruits and decorations.

NARRATOR 9: Also on New Year's Eve, children anxiously await the arrival of *Dedushka Moroz (deh-DOOSH-kah moh-ROHZ),* Grandfather Frost.

NARRATOR 10: He appears wearing a blue suit and carrying a big magic staff, handing out gifts with the assistance of the Snow Maiden.

12. Dedushka Moroz — Russia

(Kalinka)

NARRATOR 1: Beginning on December 16th, people in Venezuela attend an early Mass each day. Some people even roller skate to this service!

NARRATOR 2: This predawn service, called *Misa de Aguinaldo* (*MEE-sah day ah-gwee-NAHL-doh*) is announced by early morning firecrackers and loud ringing bells.

NARRATOR 3: Heavy sleepers have been known to tie one end of a string to their big toe, letting the other end hang out of the bedroom window.

NARRATOR 4: That way, people passing by on their way to church will pull on any leftover strings, making sure the person on the other end is awake!

NARRATOR 5: On Christmas Eve, most Venezuelans celebrate at one of nine carol services taking place during the day.

NARRATOR 6: The final Mass is at midnight, called *Misa de Gallo* (*MEE-sah day GAH-yoh*).

NARRATOR 7: Most homes feature manger scenes, but few have Christmas trees. If they do, they are normally artificial, as pine and fir trees aren't common here.

NARRATOR 8: Some nativity scenes are quite ambitious. They are called *pesebre* (*pay-SAY-bray*), and may include an elaborate scene around the manger, including mountains and valleys.

NARRATOR 9: On January 6th, "The Day of the Kings," children wake up to discover that the straw they left out beside their beds the night before is gone.

NARRATOR 10: If they've been good, gifts are in its place from *Tres Reyes* (*trace RAY-ehs*), the Three Kings, and their camels!

13. Din, Din, Din (The Journey)

Venezuela

NARRATOR 1: The main celebration in Mexico is *Las Posadas (lahs poh-SAH-dahs),* a procession that reenacts Joseph and Mary's search for shelter.

NARRATOR 2: This traditionally happens for nine nights leading up to *Nochebuena (noh-cheh-BWEH-nah)* or Christmas Eve.

NARRATOR 3: The travelers, carrying candles, are turned away at several homes, but are finally welcomed into a selected house.

NARRATOR 4: A party is held there, featuring traditional foods and a clay or paper-mâché *piñata (peen-YAH-tah),* usually shaped like a star, flower, or animal.

NARRATOR 5: Children are blindfolded, given a stick, and take turns trying to break the *piñata* open as it dangles at the end of a rope.

NARRATOR 6: Once it is broken, the children scramble for the gifts, treats, and toys which were hidden inside.

NARRATOR 7: Mexican families decorate their homes with lilies and evergreens. They cut intricate designs into brown paper bags to make a lantern called a *luminaria (loo-mee-NAH-ree-ah).*

NARRATOR 8: Then, they put sand at the bottom of each bag to weigh it down, and place a candle inside.

NARRATOR 9: These magical lights appear along sidewalks, on windowsills, and on top of walls, illuminating the community with the Christmas spirit.

NARRATOR 10: Children receive their gifts of toys and games on "The Kings' Day," the feast of the Epiphany.

14. The Search for a Room (Pedida de Posada) — Mexico

NARRATOR 1: Canada welcomes citizens from around the world, who bring their rich heritage of Christmas customs and traditions with them.

NARRATOR 2: In Newfoundland and Nova Scotia, masked mummers travel through neighborhoods, ringing bells, making a ruckus, and looking for candy.

NARRATOR 3: They wear funny disguises, and continue making noise until the host at each home can identify them!

NARRATOR 4: During Christmas week in Newfoundland, people "fish for the church," bringing their catch to be sold for the local parish.

NARRATOR 5: In Quebec, a *crèche (krehsh)* is displayed in each home. And after the midnight service, a traditional pork pie called a *tourtière (toohr-tee-EHR)* is served.

NARRATOR 6: In Ontario, Alberta, and British Columbia, Christmas trains carry riders all over the northern scenic routes, sometimes in freight trains decorated with twinkling lights.

NARRATOR 7: All over Canada, fir trees are gown. Starting in October, thousands of trees are trucked into the United States and shipped abroad.

NARRATOR 8: In Labrador, children hold lighted candles which have been placed into a hollowed-out hole in a turnip, saved from their summer harvest.

NARRATOR 9: Vancouver, in British Columbia, holds a holiday parade of ships in the harbor. The boats are decorated with lights and trees, and may even hold a singing children's choir!

NARRATOR 10: Served along with the turkey in British Columbia? How about some smoked salmon!

15. Huron Carol (Jesous Ahatonhia) — Canada

NARRATOR 1: Clement Clarke Moore's poem " 'Twas the Night Before Christmas," written in 1823, was the first to describe a jolly Santa, riding on a reindeer-driven sleigh!

NARRATOR 2: In 1863, America's version of Santa was first illustrated by Thomas Nast in an issue of *Harper's Weekly* magazine.

NARRATOR 3: In Alaska, tinsel and colored-paper wheels called "stars" are carried from door to door, while in many areas of the Southwest, the Mexican ritual of *Las Posadas (lahs poh-SAH-dahs)* takes place.

NARRATOR 4: In Philadelphia, a day-long mummers parade features string bands and strutters, wearing lavish bright-colored costumes.

NARRATOR 5: In New Orleans, a huge ox is decorated with holly and ribbons on its horns, then paraded through the streets.

NARRATOR 6: In New York, the first Tuba Christmas concert was held in 1974 at Rockefeller Plaza's Ice Rink. Today, approximately 100 cities hold similar events.

NARRATOR 7: Moravian families in Bethlehem, Pennsylvania, and Winston-Salem, North Carolina, attend the Christmas Eve "love feast," during which a large bun and cup of coffee is served to each worshipper as a token of fellowship.

NARRATOR 8: In Hawaii, Santa Claus arrives by boat! Not to be outdone, in California he catches a wave, riding in on a surf board!

NARRATOR 9: And since 1923, the grand and magnificent National Christmas Tree has been lit in Washington DC.

NARRATOR 10: Its original message of people coming together in peace and joy continues to ring true today, as we celebrate the varied customs and traditions of the Christmas season.

16. Shepherds, Go Tell! **United States**

(Rise Up, Shepherd • Go, Tell It on the Mountain)

(Segue immediately to Reprise/Bows)

17. Reprise: A World of Christmas

A World of Christmas

Holiday Songs, Carols, and Customs from 15 Countries

A Global Songbook or Program for Unison and 2-Part Voices

By Sally K. Albrecht